W9-CKI-289

IN MY BACKYARD

squirrels

by Lindsy J. O'Brien

CREATIVE EDUCATION • CREATIVE PAPERBACKS

Published by Creative Education and Creative Paperbacks
P.O. Box 227, Mankato, Minnesota 56002
Creative Education and Creative Paperbacks are imprints of
The Creative Company
www.thecreativecompany.us

Design and production by Chelsey Luther
Art direction by Rita Marshall
Printed in China

Photographs by Alamy (Jonathan Larsen/Diadem Images,
Skip Higgins of Raskal Photography, Daniel Templeton),
Corbis (Julie DeRoche/Design Pics, Doug Meek), Dreamstime
(Lukas Blazek, Mircea Costina, Eastmanphoto, Isselee, Scott
Sanders), Flickr (Rusty Clark), Getty Images (Joel Sartore),
iStockphoto (dbstudio), Shutterstock (Utekhina Anna, Bara22,
Binh Thanh Bui, IrinaK), SuperStock (FLPA/FLPA)

Library of Congress Cataloging-in-Publication Data
O'Brien, Lindsy J.
Squirrels / by Lindsy J. O'Brien.
p. cm. — (In my backyard)
Includes bibliographical references and index.
Summary: A high-interest introduction to the life cycle of
squirrels, including how kits develop, their plant-based diet,
threats from predators, and the sturdy, nested habitats of
these backyard animals.

ISBN 978-1-60818-702-7 (hardcover)
ISBN 978-1-62832-298-9 (pbk)
ISBN 978-1-56660-738-4 (eBook)
1. Squirrels—Juvenile literature.

QL737.R68 O345 2016
599.36—dc23   2015039247

CCSS: RI.1.1, 2, 3, 4, 5, 6, 7; RI.2.1, 2, 4, 5, 6, 7, 10; RF.1.1, 3, 4;
RF.2.3, 4

First Edition HC 9 8 7 6 5 4 3 2 1
First Edition PBK 9 8 7 6 5 4 3 2 1

Contents

You hear chattering above your head. A gray squirrel is sitting on a pole. The squirrel makes a "kuk-kuk-kuk" sound. It flicks its fluffy gray tail. It is communicating with you!

The animals we call "squirrels" belong to the tree squirrel group of the squirrel family.

5

When a squirrel is born, it is pink and hairless. A litter of squirrels has one to six babies. The babies are called pups or kits. Pups go off on their own after about three months.

When pups leave the litter, they do not often go farther than two miles (3.2 km) away.

Squirrels can grow to be a foot (30.5 cm) long. There are more than 200 squirrel species. Gray or red squirrels are common in backyards. Not all gray squirrels are gray in color. Some are black or white!

Black squirrels (above) mainly live in Ontario, Canada, and in some Great Lakes states.

Did you know some squirrels build nests in trees? These nests are called dreys. They are made from twigs and leaves. The nests are strong.

In winter, eastern gray squirrels (right) add mud to their dreys to keep cold air out.

Squirrels store food before winter comes. A squirrel can make thousands of caches a year! Each cache is full of seeds and nuts.

A squirrel can bury 25 nuts in an hour—and remember where each nut is.

Squirrels have many predators. Hawks, small mammals, snakes, and house pets hunt squirrels. Squirrels wave or flash their tails. This warns that danger is near. They also say "kuk-kuk-kuk." Sometimes they make a screeching call.

When a squirrel is in danger, it will run to a nearby tree and climb to safety.

Many squirrels live near people. They build nests in attics or the walls of houses. Squirrels that live near people must be careful. People are squirrel predators, too!

Squirrels active during the day provide entertainment for people and cats.

17

Squirrels can be pests, but they are fun to watch. Pay attention the next time you hear a squirrel. You might be able to understand it!

A squirrel may rest in a shady place to cool down when it is hot outside.

Activity: Squirrel Talk

Squirrels communicate with each other in many ways. They move their tails to signal danger. They make sounds to say hello. Can you figure out what a squirrel might be saying?

Materials you need: pencil, crayons or markers, and paper

Sounds Like a Squirrel

1. Take your drawing materials outside or to an open window. Choose a spot where there are trees or where you have seen squirrels before.

2. Wait, watch, and listen. If you see a squirrel, look at its tail. Is it twitching back and forth? Is it pointing straight up in the air?

3. Draw the tail. Is the squirrel signaling danger? Greeting another squirrel? Trying to warn you away from its nest? Write down what you think.

4. If the squirrel makes a sound, try to make the same sound back. Write out the sound in your journal. See if you can guess what this sound might mean.

For extra fun, when the squirrel's tail moves, make the same motion with your arms. Does the squirrel see you? Does it move its tail to answer you?

Glossary

caches: underground hiding places for food

communicating: passing information to another person or animal

litter: a group of animal babies born at the same time

mammals: animals that give birth to live young and feed them with milk

predators: animals that hunt other animals for food

species: groups of living things that are closely related

Read More

Thorington, Richard W. Jr., and Katie Ferrell. *Squirrels: The Animal Answer Guide*. Baltimore: Johns Hopkins University Press, 2006.

Zobel, Derek. *Squirrels*. Minneapolis: Bellwether Media, 2011.

Websites

DLTK's Squirrel Crafts and Activities
http://www.dltk-kids.com/animals/forest-squirrels.htm
Color pictures and make crafts of squirrels.

San Diego Zoo: Ground Squirrel
http://kids.sandiegozoo.org/animals/mammals/ground
-squirrel
Take a closer look at squirrels that live in burrows rather than nests.

Index